IQ is the yardstick by which your children will be judged throughout their lives.

This book enables you to test your children in a simple, entertaining but thoroughly scientific way, and to improve their performance.

Glenn Wilson is a New Zealander who lectures at the Institute of Psychiatry, University of London and, as visiting professor, at California State University. His books include *The Psychology of Conservatism*, *A Textbook of Human Psychology* and *Improve Your I.Q.*

After teaching for some years, Diana Grylls is now researching into child development and the components of intelligence at the Institute of Psychiatry, University of London.

Know Your Child's IQ

Glenn Wilson &
Diana Grylls

MACDONALD FUTURA PUBLISHERS

A Pocket Guide

To Kirsten and Jamie
Our first guinea pigs

Macdonald Futura Publishers Limited
Paulton House
8 Shepherdess Walk
London N1 7LW

A Pocket Guide

First published in Great Britain in 1977
Reprinted 1978, 1980

ISBN 0 7088 0982 0

Printed in Great Britain by
Hazell Watson & Viney Ltd,
Aylesbury, Bucks

Contents

Foreword

Psychologists sometimes guard their mystique quite jealously; this is not unusual among scientists. Intelligence testing is one of the areas in which psychology and the man in the street are most likely to come face to face, and consequently the mystique of intelligence testing has been guarded even more jealously here than elsewhere. Yet there are no mysteries attached to the determination of an IQ, just as there are no mysteries about taking a patient's temperature by means of a thermometer, and children and adults alike are rightly curious about just how intelligence is measured, and what it feels like to undergo the process of measurement. Oddly enough, most actually enjoy the experience; just as the body usually enjoys the experience of kicking balls, or hitting them, so the mind seems to enjoy solving puzzles, or showing off acquired knowledge. Enjoyment is therefore one of the main reasons for buying and working through books like this; but it is not the only, or even the main reason.

In our society, and probably in every advanced society that has ever existed, intelligence plays a very important part. Differences in intelligence determine to a very marked degree the position to which a person may aspire in society (even though other abilities, such as those evidenced in sport or music, painting or entertainment, may override in a few exceptional examples the effects of mediocre intelligence). Differences in intelligence determine to a large extent the kind of schooling, and the duration of schooling, optimal for a given child. It is important, therefore, to have some knowledge of one's own intelligence, and that of one's children; this knowledge, unfortunately, is difficult to obtain – you cannot go and have your IQ tested, as you might go and have your eyesight examined! It was for this purpose that I originally wrote

Know Your Own IQ and its sequel, *Check Your Own IQ*; these books enabled adults to measure their own IQ with some degree of precision, and obtain at least a rough-and-ready guide to their own mental status in this respect. The present book is an extension of this endeavour to the realm of childhood; Wilson and Grylls have put together a series of problems suitable for measuring a child's IQ, and I am sure many parents will be grateful for this help in finding out something about their child's potentialities.

Psychologists have not always welcomed endeavours of this kind as heartily as perhaps they should. They have regretted the loss of mystique, but this is not a serious complaint – mystique is not an essential part of a scientist's armoury. More serious is the problem of accuracy; IQ testing is a more difficult skill than might appear at first sight, and testing oneself or one's child obviously presents dangers. This is true, and the results should never be regarded as precise and final; they are only suggestive and give one an idea of the approximate position in the whole scale where one may be located. But self-testing is not as inaccurate as all that; results usually agree pretty well with more orthodox tests administered by trained psychologists. Provided directions are followed carefully, and scores calculated as advised, the margin of error is narrow enough to make the results meaningful.

A third criticism has been that people who tested themselves might misinterpret the results, or might become discouraged by low scores, or might get ideas above their station because of high scores. This is theoretically true, but in actual fact does not seem to have happened; nor is it likely to happen in the case of the present book. Quite the opposite is true. I have had several letters from people who discovered unexpected talents after doing the problems in my books, and went on to take university degrees and achieve other successes in fields they would not have entered at all had it not been for the results recorded on the tests. It is very much hoped that much the same may be true of this book; children have even more chances of moulding their lives than do adults, and of making correct decisions about education, work, and other aspects of their lives. For any rational decision, some knowledge of intellectual ability is essential; this book enables the worried parent to obtain a reasonable estimate of his or her child's IQ. This is important knowledge, though it is not all-important; there are other aspects of human nature which must be considered in any practical decision. But one thing at a time; knowing your own, or your child's IQ is a good, solid beginning; from there you may go on to other considerations. This book is welcome in making such rational decisions possible for many parents who otherwise would have had no access to information of this kind.

H. J. EYSENCK
Professor of Psychology, University of London

Introduction

This book has several purposes. Most obviously, it will enable parents to arrive at some estimate of how bright their child is. Many will think that they already know this. With understandable interest they have watched the intellectual progress of their offspring and no doubt concluded that they either have a moron or an exceptional genius on their hands. In either case they are likely to be wrong. For one thing, they are very emotionally involved with their own children. For another, they have limited experience of the intelligence of other children, basing their concept of what is average on other children in the family and perhaps a few other local kids. IQ tests are designed to overcome these two biases. When given strictly in accordance with instructions they produce results that are little affected by feelings and prejudices. The scores obtained by the particular child are compared with scores gained by a wide range of children of comparable age, selected not just from around the corner but from all parts of the country and representing all socioeconomic groups. This is why an IQ score may provide information which is to some degree surprising to the parent. It views the child from a suitable distance and within a more complete context.

Having a realistic appreciation of your child's intellectual capabilities may be helpful in several ways. If a child turns out to be fairly dull, certain injustices may be avoided. Accusations of laziness are unlikely to be of any use, and might be positively hurtful. Therefore they should be dropped, along with vocal expectations that the child should prepare for a career in medicine, science, the law and suchlike. He or she is unlikely to be happy or successful in intellectually demanding occupations such as these. It is better for the parents to encourage the child in other talents and interests such as music drawing, metal work, mechanics, cooking and so on – wherever the inclination of the child leads. There are a great many rewarding and socially useful pursuits that do not depend on high levels of intelligence. Awareness that a child has low IQ may protect that child from being pushed beyond his capabilities, with the consequent possibility of emotional damage.

It is also useful to know if your child is in truth a little genius. This will help in planning his future education and in pointing him towards a suitable occupation in which intelligence is fully utilized. Remember that children of high IQs appear in working class families as well as professional families, and highly intelligent parents may produce dull and mentally retarded children. It is particularly when the child's IQ is apparently out of step with his environment that parents are likely to be deceived concerning it. Some assert that IQ tests are instruments used by the middle classes for reinforcing the advantage of their own children, but the opposite is nearer to the truth. IQ tests often provide information about a child's own capabilities as distinct from those of his parents, which helps him to transcend a deprived background.

The tests in this book will also give some indication of the particular strengths and weaknesses of the child. There are five groups of problems in the pages that follow and separate scores may be obtained from them. Although these subscores are less reliable than the total IQ they do give some clue as to the child's special abilities and disabilities. For example, the vocabulary and classification tests bear on verbal ability that is important in many areas of academic achievement and certain occupations such as journalism, secretarial work and politics. Girls are particularly likely to excel in these areas. The scientific understanding and pattern completion problems draw on logical, spatial, and numerical processes that are essential to occupations such as research, navigation, design and computer programming. On average, boys do better on these skills than girls. The observation test draws on both kinds of skill and has an additional component of common sense.

Another usefulness of this book is to give children some experience with IQ tests before the time comes when important decisions hang upon their performance. It is rare for a person to go through life without being required to take an IQ test at some time or another, and the results may affect their scholastic standing, chances of getting a job, or both. Practise on the kinds of puzzles used in IQ tests may improve a person's subsequent score by up to 8 points on the scale. While this may seem small in relation to the complete scale, it could nevertheless make the difference between acceptance and rejection for a school or university, or for a desired job. Given the importance of these matters for a child's future it might be thought that parents have a duty to give their children the advantage of familiarity with the type of questions that are asked in IQ tests. Whether or not one approves of the practice of IQ testing in education and industry, the tests are being used and are likely to continue in use for a long time in the future. It is best that your children be ready to deal with them.

WHAT IS AN IQ?

IQ stands for intelligence quotient. As we have said, it is a score that tells how 'bright' a person is compared to other people. The average IQ is by definition 100; scores above 100 indicate a higher than average IQ and scores below 100 indicate a lower than average IQ. Theoretically, scores can range any amount below or above 100, but in practice, they do not meaningfully go much below 50 or above 150. These points can be taken as the approximate limits on the distribution of IQ scores. The majority of people score much closer to the 100 mark. In fact, half of the population have IQs of between 90 and 110.

If IQs don't meaningfully go much above 150, how is that some people claim very high scores like 180 or 200? Some are simply boasting, but others may have been tested as children using a method for calculating the IQ that is now largely obsolete. When the French psychologist Alfred Binet was commissioned to construct the first IQ test for school-age children he observed that as children grow older their problem solving powers increase. This suggested to him the idea of 'mental age'. A child with a mental age of, say, ten year old was one who could equal the scores of an average ten year old on Binet's tests, whatever his actual (chronological) age might be. The first IQ scores were calculated as a ratio of mental age over chronological age, and multiplied by 100 to remove the decimal point. For example, a ten year old child with a mental age of 13 would have an IQ of 130, while a ten year old child with a mental age of 7 would have an IQ of 70. IQs calculated in this way may be extremely high (or low), particularly when the denominator (age in years) is very low. Thus a one-year-old baby who does as well on tests as an average two-year-old comes out with an IQ of 200. This figure may then be quoted by his parents, and subsequently himself, well into his adult years when it has ceased to be valid.

The ratio method of calculating IQs breaks down completely in adulthood, when the mental age is fairly steady though chronological age moves on relentlessly. IQ tests now use a statistical method of calculating IQs, based on the rarity of a person's deviation from average. An IQ of 120 implies that the testee is brighter than 90% of the population, while 140 puts a person ahead of 99% of people. A person with an IQ of 80 is brighter than only 10% of people, and only a few score less than 60.

The concept of intelligence stems from the fact that mental skills of nearly every kind are positively linked so that if you are clever at one thing you are probably clever at others. If a person has a good memory there is a better than even chance that he has a good vocabulary, and that he is good at arithmetic. Similarly, if a person is good at arithmetic he probably also has a good memory and vocabulary. These associations do not always hold true, but they do on average, and this is what is meant by saying that all abilities are intercorrelated. IQ tests try to get at this general ability by sampling performance on different kinds of intellectual tasks and taking an overall average.

Some tests give separate scores for a variety of specific abilities such as general knowledge, vocabulary, verbal reasoning, verbal fluency, numerical ability, spatial reasoning, mechanical ability, perceptual speed, memory and so on. This is of theoretical interest and has practical application in areas such as vocational guidance and the diagnosis of brain damage and specific disabilities. Nevertheless, different abilities are so closely linked that an overall measure of general intelligence is of much broader usefulness. In particular it is a very good indication of how well a person will do in a course of higher education. A minimum IQ of 120 is probably necessary for a basic university degree, and it would be difficult to obtain a higher degree with an IQ of less than 130. The only other good predictor of academic success is the individual's previous academic record, but this is limited because it lacks standardization. It is hard to compare marks, grades and references given by different instructors and different institutions, whereas IQ scores are directly comparable no matter which school you come from.

The IQ gives a good indication of the occupational group that a person will end up in, though not of course the specific occupation. Some occupations typical of various IQ levels are:

140	Top Civil Servants; Professors and Research Scientists.
130	Physicians and Surgeons; Lawyers; Engineers (Civil and Mechanical).
120	School Teachers; Pharmacists; Accountants; Nurses; Stenographers; Managers.
110	Foremen; Clerks; Telephone Operators; Salesmen; Policemen; Electricians.
100+	Machine Operators; Shopkeepers; Butchers; Welders; Sheet Metal Workers.
100—	Warehousemen; Carpenters; Cooks and Bakers; Small Farmers; Truck and Van Drivers.

Labourers; Gardeners; Upholsterers; Farmhands;
       Miners; Factory Packers and Sorters.

It is widely thought that the connection between intelligence
and occupation comes about because of the educational oppor-
tunities that intelligent parents are able to offer their children.
In other words, many people believe that intelligence is a re-
flection of social class rather than the other way about. There
is some truth to this, but research shows that our intelligence
'causes' our social class much more powerfully than the social
class of our parents 'causes' our intelligence. The connection
between IQ and occupation shown above is not circular, for
IQ measures in childhood will predict which children within
a family will rise in the social scale and which will fall in relation to the position of their parents. Although IQ is not the
only factor determining occupational success, most jobs have
a minimum intellectual requirement which must be met before
other qualities begin to count.

RELIABILITY OF THE IQ

What are the chances that one would get the same IQ score
if tested again on another occasion? The measurement of intelligence is always subject to some error. Since it is based on
a sample of one's mental prowess, its stability depends on the
adequacy of that sample. Obviously, the greater the amount
of performance that is sampled (i.e. the longer the test) the
more reliable is the IQ that is obtained. The best IQ tests,
properly conducted, take more than an hour and give confidence limits of about plus or minus 5 points. That is, with a
fair degree of confidence it can be said that the 'true' IQ will
not be more than 5 points removed from the figure obtained.
For all practical purposes this is a very high degree of accuracy. If a person is thinking of undertaking a university
course it matters little whether his IQ is 90 or 95. He would
be well advised to forget it. Likewise, it would make little
odds whether his IQ was 130 or 135. Any difficulties he en-
countered would more likely be due to other factors such as
personality or motivation, not intelligence.

A limitation on the reliability of the IQs obtained with this book is that of the age of testing. The younger the child is when tested the less sure we can be of predicting his adult IQ. In fact, attempts to measure IQ below the age of 4 or 5 have failed almost completely. This is because the skills measured in infancy draw mainly on physical maturation processes which are virtually unrelated to the complex mental skills comprising adult intelligence. Remember that an infant ape learns to walk earlier than a human baby – this does not make it more intelligent. The problems used in this book draw on skills such as vocabulary and abstract reasoning which are known to be basic to intelligence, and they stretch to ages as young as it is possible to get useful measures. Still, we can place greater faith in the scores obtained by children of 10 and 11 than those of children, of 5 or 6.

VALIDITY

The question of validity is concerned with whether the tests are really measuring what they are supposed to measure. Do they really measure intelligence, something else, or perhaps nothing at all? This is a complex question, but it is partly answered by the fact that IQ scores help in predicting educational and occupational success. This is the main purpose for which they are designed, and they do it very well. What is more, they are not themselves markedly affected by general educational achievement. Coaching on the actual test items will of course give a person an advantage, and practise on similar test items will also raise the IQ score by a few points. But once experience with the testing materials has been controlled the IQ score will not be affected by education to any great extent.

There are a number of assumptions in IQ testing, which if violated would lead to invalid results. Verbal tests obviously assume that the testee speaks the language in which the test is written. Immigrant children sometimes do badly on IQ tests not because they are dull, but because they are not fluent in English. IQ tests also assume that the subject is motivated to do well. This assumption sometimes breaks down, e.g. when an individual is taking the test as part of a job selection programme in which he knows that people with 'too much' intelligence are rejected as unlikely to stick at the job. In addition, excessively high motivation could produce a degree of anxiety which is debilitating to test performance.

Generally, IQ tests show adequate reliability and validity when well-designed tests are used by properly qualified psychologists under suitable conditions of testing. Note that these conditions are not met fully in the tests that follow since unqualified parents will be conducting them. This means that they should be treated only as a *guide* to the IQ of the child – an estimate which should be checked by a qualified psychologist before any important decisions are based upon it.

IS IQ INHERITED OR DUE TO UPBRINGING?

Although many laymen are disposed to doubt it for one reason or another, psychologists now know that the major part of variation in intelligence (about 80%) is due to heredity. The environment plays a definite but relatively small part. Several different lines of evidence point to this conclusion with results that agree remarkably well. Best known, are the studies that make use of twins. Identical twins result from a single egg which has split after fertilization. Therefore they share common heredity. The effect of the environment on intelligence can be gauged by comparing the IQs of such twins who have been brought up separately from each other. On average their IQs differ by $6\frac{1}{2}$ points which is only about 2 points greater than the difference to be expected when the same person is tested on two occasions. In other words, differences in upbringing and other life experiences add only about 2 points on average to the IQ difference between identical twins.

A second important comparison is that between identical twins and fraternal (two-egg) twins. 'Frats', like ordinary brothers and sisters (called sibs), share only 50% of heredity compared to the 100% for 'ids'. If IQ is influenced by heredity we would expect the correlation between ids to be higher than that for frats. This is found to be the case. On average, identical twins correlate ·86, fraternal twins ·55 a substantial difference which indicates that IQ is strongly influenced by heredity.

Another fairly striking indication of the inheritance of IQ is the phenomenon of *regression towards the mean*. Children of high IQ parents show, on average, a lower intelligence than their parents, while children of dull parents tend to be brighter than their parents. This regression effect is observed in all genetically mediated variables, for example height, and it is hard to imagine how it could be explained in environmentalist terms. If environmental influences are dominant, class based advantage and disadvantage should be cumulative. Bright parents would provide optimum environments for their children who would then grow up brighter than themselves, and dull parents would cause a further downward drift in their children's IQs by failing to provide a stimulating home. Instead, the reverse occurs, which suggests that extremely bright and dull children are produced by unusual gene combinations that are unstable and easily broken down in the intergeneration reshuffle.

Studies of the intelligence of orphan children have also proved useful in relation to the nature-nurture controversy. Orphanage conditions expose children to a relatively uniform environment. They have the same teachers, food, buildings, companions, games, excursions and books. If high and low IQs stem from good and bad environments respectively, then removing the extremes of environment in this way should produce fairly uniform IQs. In fact only a very minor reduction in the amount of variation is observed (less than 10%), again demonstrating the importance of heredity.

Perhaps most convincing of all is the finding that foster children correlate in IQ with their biological mothers to about the same extent as children brought up by their own mothers, while correlations with their foster mothers are almost non-existent. The particular characteristics of the foster home apparently make little difference. Factors such as socioeconomic status, number of books, amount of time devoted to the child, and pressure for education, which are often said to be important, have been studied and found to make only marginal contributions to the IQ of the foster children.

All this evidence allows us to make a fairly firm estimate of 80% heritability for the IQ. Environmental effects are confirmed, but their contribution amounts to only about 20% of variation. It is not possible to be too precise with these percentages because they depend to some extent on the kinds of hereditary and environmental extremes that are permitted in the calculation. Certain kinds of mental deficiency such as mongolism have a very simple genetic basis and yield IQs so low that they fall outside of the normal distribution. If these were included in the formulae, the proportion of variation due to inheritance would appear as higher still. On the other hand, there are various extreme kinds of environmental intervention such as head injury or solitary confinement which, if included in the formulae, would significantly inflate the environmental influence. The figure of 80% heritability refers to the relative effects of the normal ranges of genes and environment.

SEX DIFFERENCES

Overall, the IQ scores of men and women come out pretty well the same, and have done since the earliest days of test construction (well before emancipation of women). However, there are two interesting sex differences in intelligence. Firstly, men show a greater amount of dispersion; there are more very bright men and more very dull ones. This finding is understandable if we assume that some of the genes that determine intelligence are carried on the X chromosome; males have little genetic material on their Y chromosome with which to offset errors or extremes contributed by their mother. That might explain why males are over-represented in institutions for the mentally subnormal on the one hand, and produce more works of creative genius on the other. But men are also more highly driven both by biological constitution and the demands of society. Such pressures might partly account for their high productivity and drop-out rate.

The second difference between men and women in intelligence concerns the particular abilities in which they excel. In general, women are superior in language skills such as verbal fluency and vocabulary, in rote memory, and manual dexterity; men are superior in visuo-spatial problems, mathematics and reasoning. Evidence for a biological basis to these sex differences comes from studies of animals where parallel differences have been observed between male and female rats and other mammals. Developmental studies reveal that differences between boys and girls appear within a few months of birth which seem basic to the differences in adulthood. For example, right from the start girls show greater interest in sound patterns and boys in visual stimuli. Since linguistic skills are handled primarily by the left hemisphere of the brain while visuo-spatial skills are mediated more in the right, this ties in with the observation that neuroanatomical development is more advanced in the left hemisphere of young girls and the right hemisphere of boys.

It seems likely that the specialization of abilities in men and women has an evolutionary origin. In mammals generally, the males tend to roam around for purposes of hunting, aggression and defence. The females stay at home tending offspring and so do not require the same visuo-spatial ability. These differences probably also help to explain the different occupations into which males and females drift. Thus men predominate in occupations requiring mathematical, mechanical, and spatial skills, e.g. engineers and airline pilots (apart from jobs requiring sheer physical strength) while women predominate in secretarial and assembly jobs, where their superior linguistic and manual skills are appropriate.

CREATIVITY AND GENIUS

Many parents will wish to know whether these tests can tell if their child is a potential genius. Unfortunately the answer is no. Prediction of creativity and genius requires more than a measure of intelligence. Having a high IQ is probably a prerequisite but is not in itself sufficient. Personality and motivational factors are no doubt also important. Attempts have been made to design specific tests of creativity, but they fail on two counts. First, they correlate so highly with ordinary IQ tests that doubts are raised as to whether they measure anything different. Second, they usually fail to distinguish truly creative individuals (people who have actually demonstrated their creative ability by what they have produced) from those who are not.

Standard IQ tests are primarily designed to measure important differences around the middle of the population. We know little about the differences between people who score say 140 and 150 because there are so few of them around that comparative studies cannot easily be done. In any case, most of the tests have a definite ceiling in that a number of individuals get all or nearly all of the problems correct and cannot therefore be distinguished one from another. People of acknowledged genius might be distinguished by exceptionally high IQs but the tests that we commonly use are not geared to making fine distinctions at the extreme ends of the distribution. Since the so-called tests of creativity don't seem to do any better, at the moment we have to admit that it is not possible to assess or predict creative genius by means of psychological tests.

MENTAL SUBNORMALITY

IQ tests are successful in diagnosing subnormality. In fact, they reveal the existence of two kinds. There are people with IQs between about 60 and 80 who apparently represent the bottom end of the normal distribution. These children are sometimes called *familial* retardates because they tend to come from homes where the parents and siblings are also of low IQ. Then there is another group of even lower IQ (usually about 30 to 60). They may come from any sort of home and their parents show a similar range of IQs to those of the normal population. This type of mental retardation is due to an *organic disorder* of some kind – brain injury or lack of oxygen at birth, chromosome anomalies such as mongolism and Turner's syndrome, and single gene disorders which, because they are recessive, have been passed on by parents who did not themselves appear defective. The presence of this group in the population causes a small bump at the bottom end of what would otherwise be a fairly even bell-shaped distribution of IQ scores.

There is no equivalent abnormality detectable by standard IQ tests yielding a bump at the top half of the distribution that might be labelled 'freaky genius'. However, some researchers think that certain autistic and idiot-savant children represent variants of extremely high intelligence. These are children who show intellectual impairment in many areas and often a lack of interest in social communication, yet they have outstanding talent in certain highly specialized areas such as music and mathematics. Such children are apparently more likely to come from high IQ parents than are normal children. Theories which blame parental coldness and childhood experiences for these conditions are no longer widely entertained.

HOW TO USE THIS BOOK

Five tests of different aspects of intelligence now follow. In each case they are preceded by instructions as to how they should be administered to the child. If you need to know anything about scoring before the test is given, this will also be described in the instructions. These instructions must be kept to exactly, otherwise the results will not be valid. It will be necessary to resist the strong and very human temptation to help the child do his very best by offering little prompts and cues. This is strictly inadmissible except where explicitly called for in the instructions. Only if the tests are given in the standard form will the norms at the back have any validity; and if the norms are not valid then neither is the IQ score based on them.

At the end of each test instructions are given for calculating the total score and comparing it with typical scores obtained by children of the same age. These separate subscores are not called IQs. The term is reserved for an average taken over several different types of mental skill. They are, however, equivalent in that they tell whether the child is advanced or retarded for his age, and they all contribute to the final overall intelligence score. The method for calculating and interpreting this is described in a concluding note.

Remember, do not prompt and push the child, and do not tell him when he is right or wrong. You may go through the answers with him later after the test is finished if he is interested or if you wish to use it as an educational exercise, but these purposes cannot be mixed simultaneously. Especially with young children it will be necessary to reassure them that the puzzles get progressively difficult and that most of them are really for much older children. In most cases the instructions will say to stop the test if a lot of failures occur in a row. Some of the tests must be given orally without the child looking at the book; for others the child should be given the book and allowed to work in his own time. The instructions will make this clear. It will usually not be possible to work through all the tests at one sitting; it is a good idea to distribute them over several evenings or the whole of a weekend.

Test I: Vocabulary

INSTRUCTIONS FOR GIVING THE TEST

On the following pages are a series of
puzzles designed to test the child's
vocabulary. Each puzzle consists of four
pictures and the child has to indicate which
one corresponds to the test word. For each
puzzle read the word out aloud and ask the
child to point to the picture which best
illustrates it. Put a ring around the letter
code of the picture chosen. Encourage him
to guess if he does not know the meaning of
the word, but stop the test if five
consecutive mistakes occur.

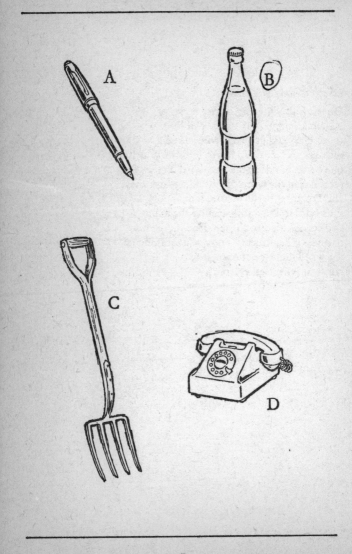

A

B

C

D

A

B

C

D

A

B

C

D

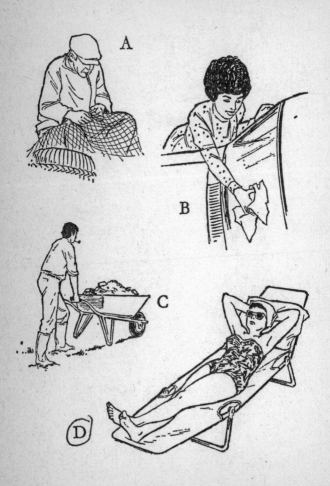

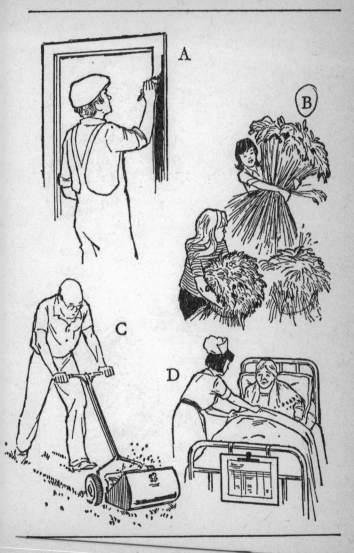

A

B

C

D

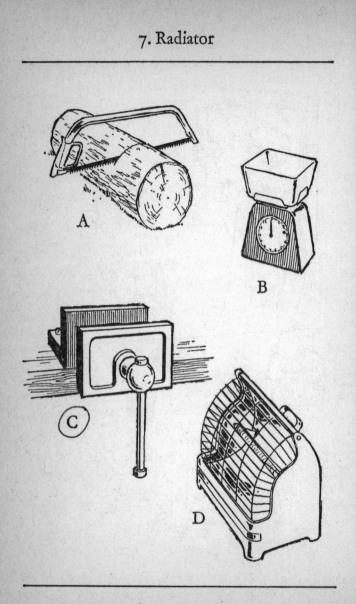

A

B

C

D

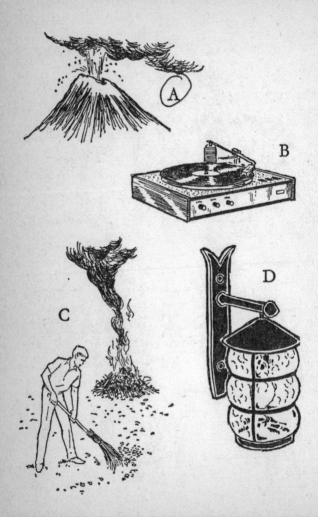

A

B

C

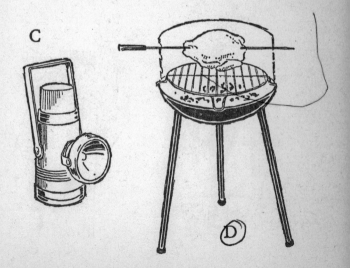

D

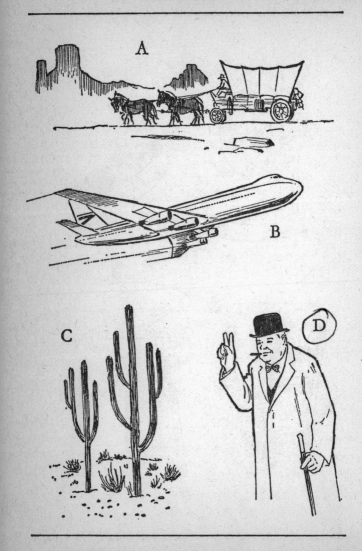

A

B

C

D

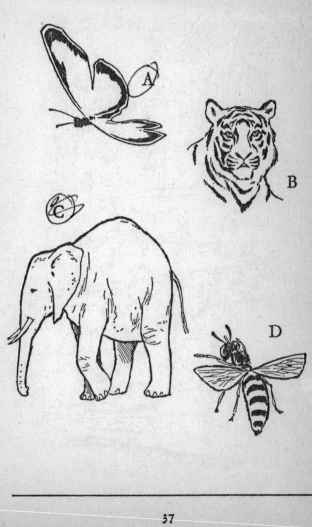

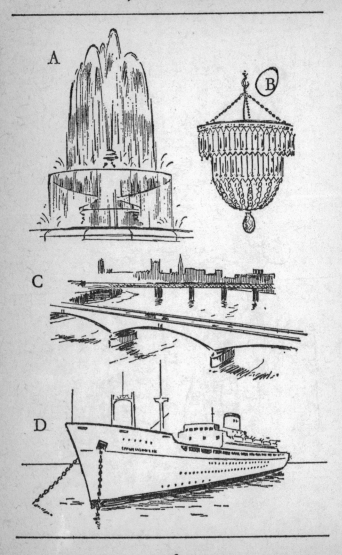

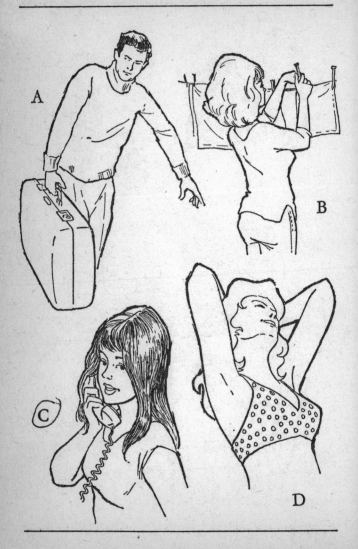

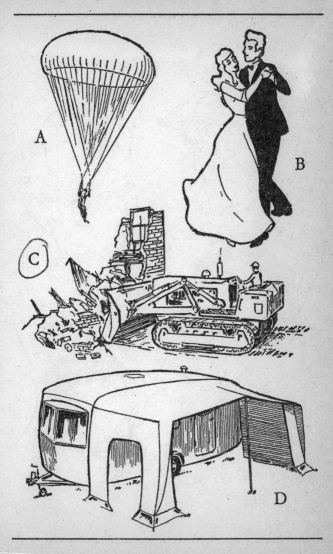

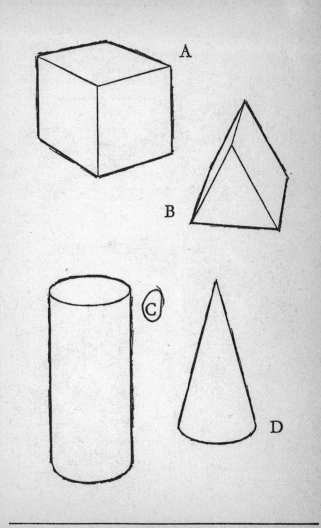

A

B

C

D

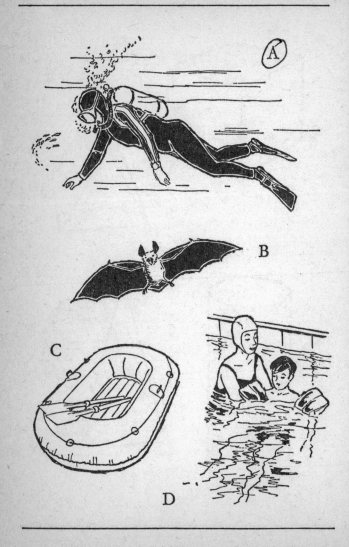

A

B

C

D

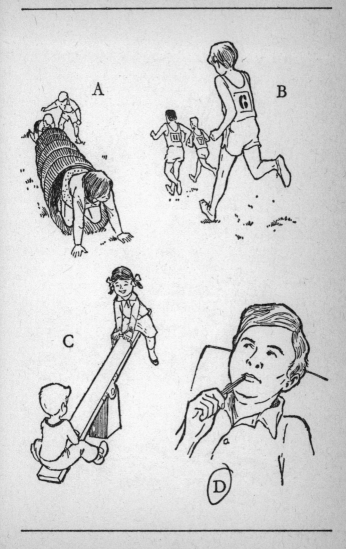

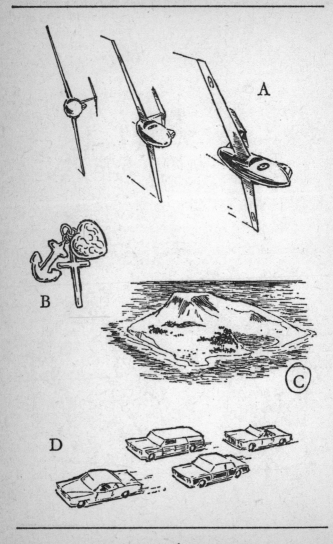

A

B

C

D

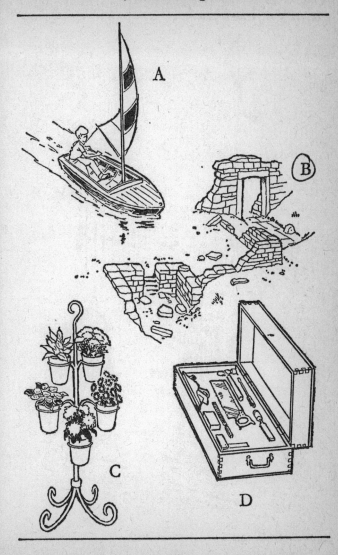

A

B

C

D

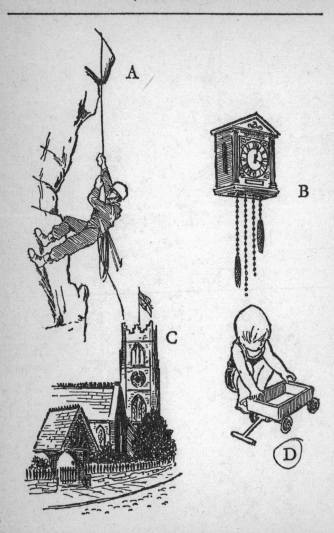

A

B

C

D

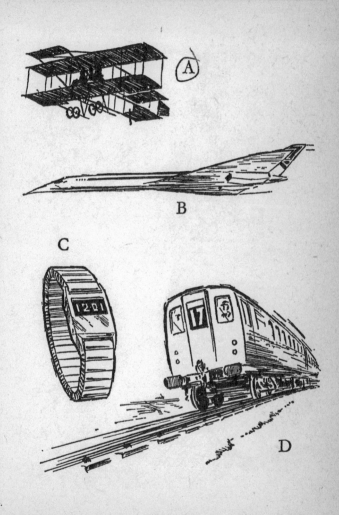

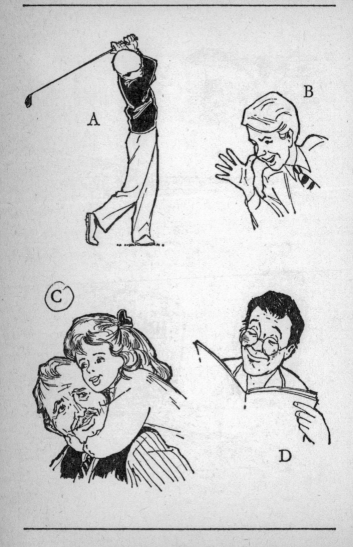

A

B

C

D

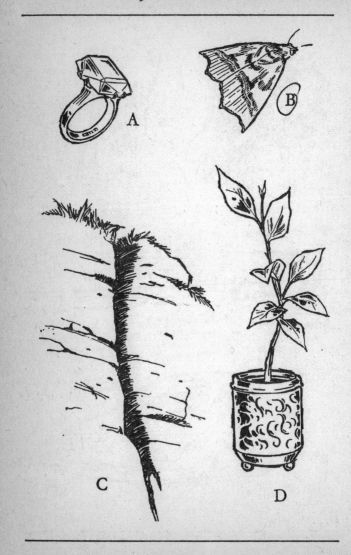

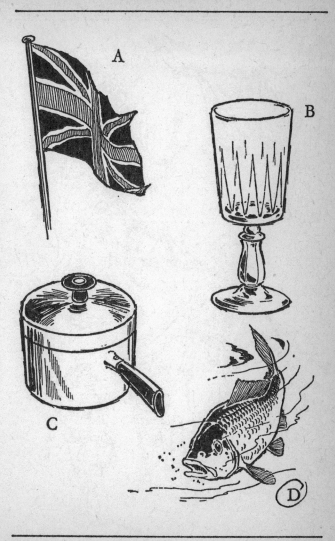

A

B

C

D

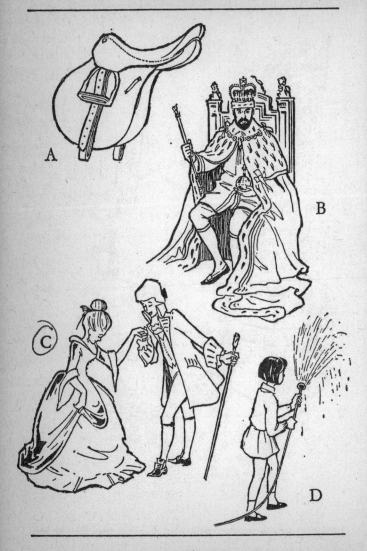

A

B

C

D

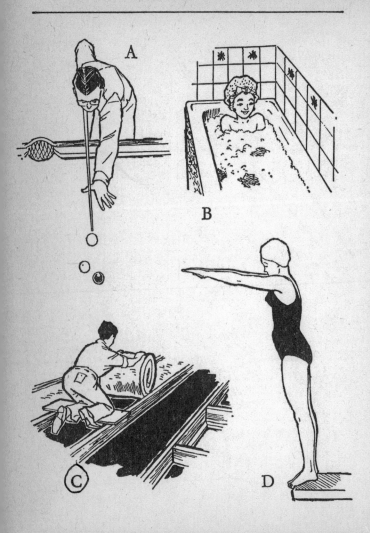

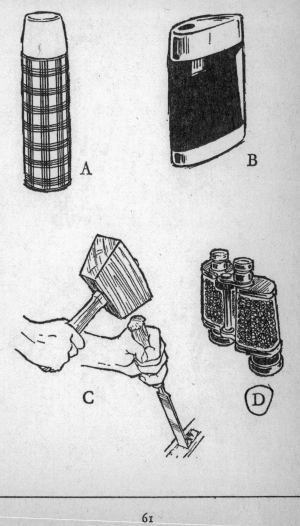

A

B

C

D

A

B

C

D

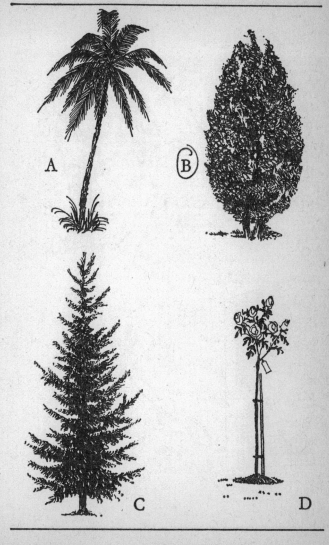

A

B

C

D

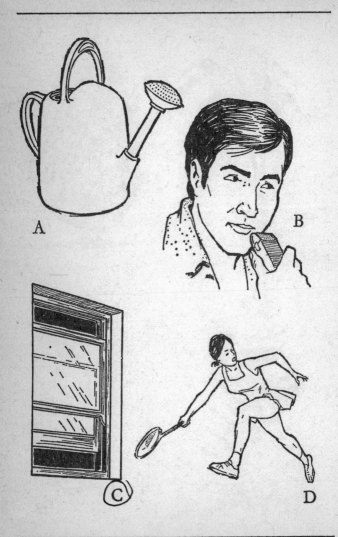

A

B

C

D

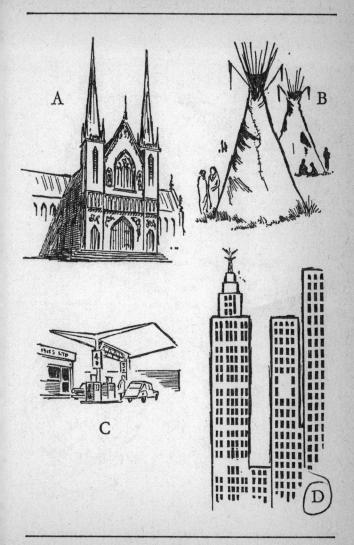

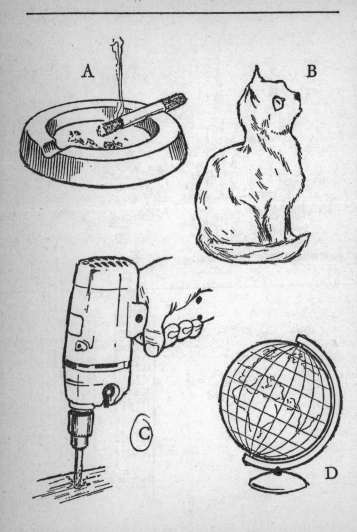

Scoring for Test I

CORRECT ANSWERS ARE:

1 b, 2 d, 3 c, 4 d, 5 d, 6 b, 7 d, 8 c, 9 a, 10 d,
11 d, 12 c, 13 a, 14 b, 15 b, 16 d, 17 c, 18 c,
19 d, 20 c, 21 a, 22 d, 23 a, 24 b, 25 a, 26 b,
27 a, 28 a, 29 c, 30 a, 31 c, 32 a, 33 b, 34 c,
35 b, 36 b, 37 c, 38 d, 39 b, 40 a, 41 d, 42 c,
43 c, 44 a, 45 a.

Add up the number of correct answers. If
the test was stopped before completion
because of five consecutive failures, add $\frac{1}{4}$ of
the number of non-attempted items (which
we would expect to be correct by chance).
Refer the total score thus obtained to the
table below to arrive at a 'vocabulary
quotient' according to the child's age. If the
score is uneven take it as halfway between
the two adjacent table entries. Refer to the
last chapter for interpretation of the
quotient.

VOCABULARY QUOTIENTS

SCORE	AGE 5*	6	7	8	9	10	11
10—	60—	60—	60—	60—	60—	60—	60—
12	70	65	63	61	60	60—	60—
14	90	80	75	71	69	66	65
16	102	93	85	80	76	74	72
18	115	103	95	88	84	80	77
20	127	113	103	96	90	86	83
22	136	123	111	103	96	91	87
24	143	131	120	109	103	97	92
26	151	139	128	117	108	103	97
28		145	135	125	116	108	103
30		152	141	132	123	114	107
32			147	137	128	120	113
34			154	144	134	126	119
36				149	140	132	124
38				156	146	137	130
40					150	143	136
42						148	142
44						155	150+

* Use this column for age range 5 yrs 0 mths to 5 yrs 11 mths; similarly for the other columns. In other words, the true reference points for these columns are $5\frac{1}{2}$ yrs, $6\frac{1}{2}$ yrs, etc.

Test II: Classification

INSTRUCTIONS FOR GIVING THE TEST

There follows a series of problems designed to test the child's ability to use generalizations and categories. Each problem consists of a list of words which all share something in common except for one. The child's task is to identify the odd one out. If the child can read the words he may be allowed to work through the problems at his own pace. If he cannot read them they should be read out aloud in such a way as not to betray the odd word by inflexion, and repeated as often as the child requests. Accept the first answer that is offered and do not tell the child whether he is right or wrong. Once again the problems get progressively difficult, so stop the test if five successive failures occur.

PUT A LINE THROUGH THE ODD ONE OUT

1. cat, dog, ~~house~~

2. hat, ~~bicycle~~, coat

3. ~~tree~~, cake, biscuit

4. knife, fork, spoon, ~~boat~~

5. pencil, crayon, pen, ~~garden~~

6. chair, table, ~~spider~~, cupboard

7. hand, arm, ~~television~~, leg

8. piglet, puppy, kitten, ~~cow~~

9. boots, ~~gloves~~, slippers, shoes, socks

10. crying, laughing, ~~sitting~~, smiling, frowning

11. elbow, knee, ~~tooth~~, finger, neck

12. cuckoo, eagle, ~~bee~~, robin, sparrow

13. rose, ~~elm~~, daisy, tulip, dandelion

14. January, ~~Spring~~, December, April, August

15. clouds, wind, tornado, ~~mountain~~, hurricane

16. ~~avalanche~~, seal, Eskimo, polar bear, walrus

17. ribs, ~~collarbone~~, skull, spine, heart

18. pansy, oak, bee, ~~well~~, snail

19. square, rectangle, triangle, hexagon, ~~cube~~

20. mother, grandmother, father, daughter, ~~sister~~

72

21. pork, ~~venison~~, cod, beef, mutton

22. panther, tiger, lion, leopard, ~~zebra~~, cheetah

23. swan, cork, pebble, log, ~~dinghy~~, duck

24. thistle, weasel, holly, porcupine, gorse, <u>hedgehog</u>.

25. ~~windmill~~, yacht, weathercock, liner, kite

26. star, meteor, comet, planet, ~~astronaut~~, asteroid

27. Julius Caesar, Oliver Cromwell, Abraham Lincoln, ~~Tchaikovsky~~, Lenin

28. plateau, valley, canyon, gorge, ~~crevasse~~

29. turtle, crocodile, dolphin, lizard, ~~snake~~

30. Alps, Nile, <u>Himalayas</u>, Andes, Rockies, Caucasians

31. otter, seal, <u>frog</u>, turtle, fish, crocodile

32. pearl, ruby, sapphire, emerald, <u>diamond</u>

33. Michelangelo, Marco Polo, Columbus, Drake, <u>Livingstone</u>

34. trumpet, trombone, bugle, tambourine, tuba, <u>French horn</u>

35. rubber, nylon, cotton, leather, <u>jute</u>

36. <u>Archimedes</u>, Darwin, Edison, Newton, Einstein, Napoleon

37. fir, elm, <u>ash</u>, chestnut, birch

38. turtle, kangaroo, mole, deer, rat, <u>whale</u>

39. Renoir, <u>Van Gogh</u>, Cezanne, Mozart, Picasso, Dali

40. peals, lapse, leaps, sleep, <u>pleas</u>

Scoring for Test II

CORRECT ANSWERS ARE:

1. house, 2. bicycle, 3. tree, 4. boat, 5. garden, 6. spider,
7. television, 8. cow, 9. gloves, 10. sitting, 11. tooth, 12. bee,
13. elm, 14. spring, 15. mountain, 16. avalanche, 17. heart,
18. well, 19. cube, 20. father, 21. cod, 22. zebra, 23. pebble,
24. weasel, 25. liner, 26. astronaut, 27. Tchaikovsky,
28. plateau, 29. dolphin, 30. Nile, 31. fish, 32. pearl,
33. Michelangelo, 34. tambourine, 35. nylon, 36. Napoleon,
37. fir, 38. turtle, 39. Mozart, 40. sleep.

Add up the correct answers plus $\frac{1}{5}$ the no. of non-attempted items, and refer the total to the table below.

CLASSIFICATION QUOTIENTS

SCORE	AGE 5*	6	7	8	9	10	11
6	66—	64—	62—	60—			
8	76	72	69	67	65	62	
10	85	80	76	73	70	68	66
12	95	87	83	78	76	73	71
14	105	95	88	84	81	77	75
16	115	104	96	90	86	83	79
18	125	112	103	96	91	87	84
20	135	122	110	102	96	92	88
22	147	130	118	109	102	96	92
24	160	141	126	116	107	101	96
26		152	136	124	114	107	100
28			147	132	121	113	106
30				141	128	119	111
32				152	137	126	117
34					146	133	124
36					156	140	130
38						150	137
40							145+

* Use this column for age range 5 yrs 0 mths to 5 yrs 11 mths.

Test III: Observation

INSTRUCTIONS FOR GIVING THE TEST

This test consists of a series of pictures which contain some error or omission. The task of the child is to locate and say what is missing or wrong with the picture. Score each response either right or wrong on a separate sheet of paper so that the child does not get feedback concerning his correctness. If the child gives a wrong response on any item say 'Yes, anything else?' the first time only; if a second incorrect answer is given, or if no answer is forthcoming within about a minute, mark the item wrong and go on to the next one. Correct answers are given at the end of the test. All 35 items should be worked through regardless of the number of successive errors.

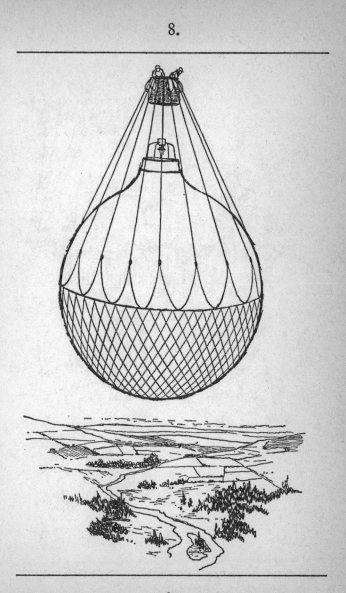

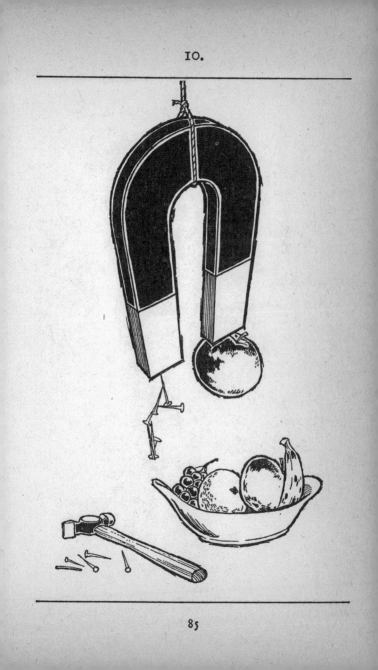

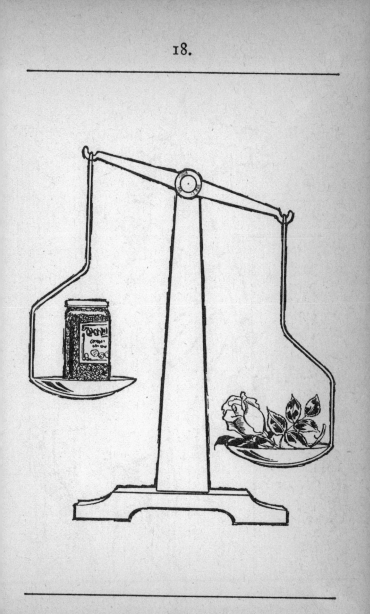

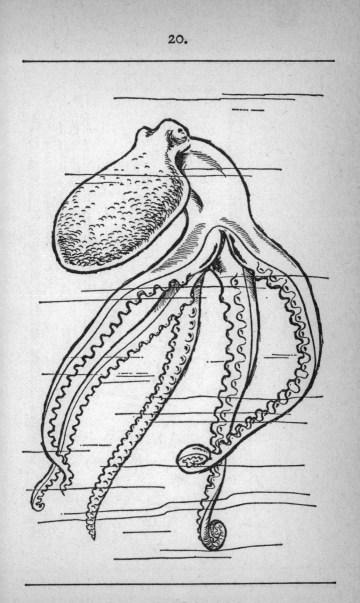

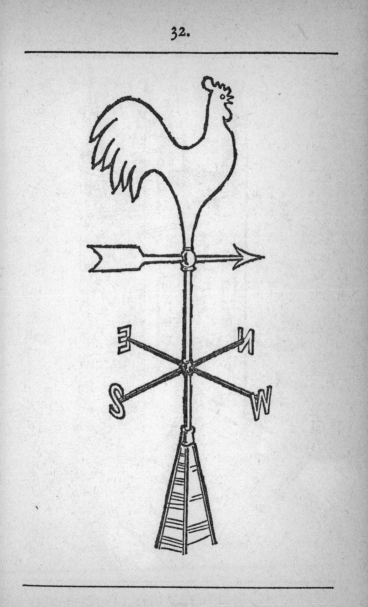

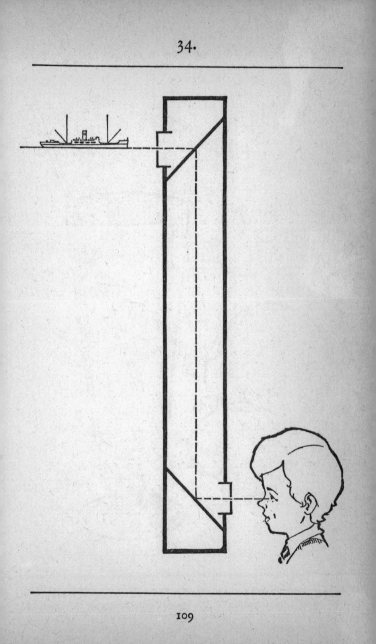

Scoring for Test III

CORRECT ANSWERS ARE:

1. Ears missing, 2. Handle of wheelbarrow, 3. Butterfly should not be in fish bowl, 4. Dial on telephone, 5. Football boot on left foot, 6. Spokes on front wheel, 7. Trigger unit, 8. Balloon upside down, 9. Hippopotamus not a farm animal, 10. Magnets do not attract fruit, 11. Hedgehogs do not climb trees, 12. Pears do not grow on holly, 13. Comb on rooster, 14. Gun is anachronistic, 15. Numbers on clockface, 16. Mirror image should be same as original plant, 17. Barometer reading inconsistent with weather, 18. Jam should outweigh rose, 19. Left hoof should not be cloven, 20. Octopus has eight legs, 21. Top of door would not fit doorway, 22. Direction of smoke vs. trees, 23. Golf clubs as ski sticks, 24. Thermometer reading unlikely, 25. Should be four strings on violin, 26. Should be two sets of tracks in snow, 27. May has 31 days, 28. One flag blowing in wrong direction. 29. Water levels should be equal, 30. Submarine does not have smoke stack, 31. Light should not be on as key is not closed. 32. East and west reversed, 33. Clock and sundial give inconsistent readings, 34. Top mirror at wrong angle for effective periscope action, 35. Straw should appear bent because of refraction.

Add up the number of correct responses and
refer the total thus obtained to the table
below to arrive at an 'observation quotient'
for the child. Refer to the last chapter of the
book for interpretation of this quotient.

OBSERVATION QUOTIENTS

SCORE	AGE 5*	6	7	8	9	10	11
4	78	68					
6	84	76	69	62			
8	90	83	76	69	66	62	
10	97	88	82	75	70	66	63
12	103	95	87	80	74	70	67
14	108	101	93	86	78	74	70
16	116	107	98	92	84	78	74
18	123	114	105	97	90	83	77
20	130	122	111	103	95	88	82
22	136	130	120	109	100	94	87
24	143	137	129	118	107	99	93
26	149	144	137	128	116	105	97
28		150	144	137	127	114	102
30			152	146	137	125	112
32				154	148	138	125
34					157	150	140+

* Use this column for age range 5 yrs 0 mths to 5 yrs 11 mths.

Test IV: Scientific understanding

INSTRUCTIONS FOR GIVING THE TEST

Below are a number of questions designed
to tap the child's awareness of and curiosity
about the world around him and his
comprehension of the natural principles
underlying it. Read the question out aloud
and score the answer 0, 1, or 2 depending on
which of the example answers is closest.
Note that if alternative answers are given
the child need only produce one of them to
score the points assigned. Do not prompt or
cross-examine the child except for the
specific probes indicated in the scoring, and
don't tell him whether he is right or wrong.
Again, you can go over the correct answers
later if you like. Stop the test if the child
fails to get any points for five consecutive
questions.

N.B. Do not read out the alternative answers
to the child. They are there only as a guide
to scoring. The child must answer the
questions spontaneously.

1. **Where does wool come from ?**

2 Sheep
1 Australia/New Zealand
o A shop
  The sewing room

2. **What do you need to make ice ?**

2 Water and low
    temperatures
1 A refrigerator
  Cold water
o An ice-tray

3. **Why do hedgehogs have prickles ?**

2 Protection from enemies
1 To stop you picking them
    up
o To fight with

4. **Why are there no trees in a desert ?**

2 Too dry
  Lack of rain
1 Climate no good (probe
    'Why not?')
o Too hot
  Soil no good
  All burned down/been
    chopped down

5. **Where do pearls come from ?**

2 Oysters
1 The sea
  A shell (probe 'What
    kind?')
o Necklaces

6. **Where does the Sun go at night ?**

2 The other side of the
    world
  Below the horizon
1 Under the ground
  Down behind the hills/
    buildings/trees
o Behind the clouds
  Heaven
  Somebody turns it off

7. **Why do some balloons float up in the air ?**

2 Filled with gas that is
    lighter than air
  Filled with hydrogen/
    helium
1 Filled with gas (probe
    'What kind?')
o Pumped up very full of air
  Owner let go of the string

8. Why could we not live on the Moon without a space suit?

2 No oxygen/atmosphere for us to breathe
   Extremes of heat and cold because no atmospheric insulation

1 Could not breathe (probe 'Why not?')
   Would burn up/freeze (probe 'Why?')

0 Would float away into space
   No water to drink
   Monsters would kill us

9. How does a parachute slow us down when we are falling?

2 Creates air resistance
   Collects a lot of air underneath which drags against it

1 The air rushes into it

0 It opens up wide
   The man is tied on with strings

10. How do scientists know what kind of animal lived millions of years ago?

2 Study of fossils/bones preserved in certain kinds of rock

1 Digging up remains from under the ground
   Cave drawings

0 Reading lots of books
   Talking to primitive tribes that can remember them

11. Why do we need blood in our body?

2 Delivery of oxygen and nourishment to organs
   Carries auto-immune system (anti-bodies etc.)
   Elimination of waste products

1 To stay alive (probe 'Be more specific')

0 Otherwise we bleed to death
   So we look pink

12. Why does throwing sand on a campfire put it out?

2 Fires cannot burn without air/oxygen
   The sand extinguishes the flame by cutting off the supply of air

1 It smothers the flame (probe 'How does it do that?')

0 Because the sand is wet
   It knocks the flames off the pieces of wood

13. How is a rainbow formed?

2 Differential refraction of
   sunlight through
   raindrops
   Spectral dispersion of
   white light
   Raindrops act like little
   prisms to produce
   different colours

, 1 Sunlight shining through
   raindrops
   It's what happens when
   the sun's rays pass
   through mist

0 Sun shining on the clouds
   God sends it to say there'll
   never be another flood

14. Why do chameleons change colour?

• 2 Camouflage
   So enemies cannot see
   them against their
   background

1 Protection

0 They are shy/emotionally
   disturbed
   They like variety – like
   people change their
   clothes

15. How does an X–ray machine help doctors to see inside the body?

2 The rays pass through
   some parts of the body
   easier than others and
   the pattern emerging on
   the other side is picked
   up on a photographic
   plate

1 The rays go through
   everything but bone
   Rays go through people
   and are photographed
   when they come out

0 Like a camera that sees
   through people
   Like the six million dollar
   man can see through
   people

16. Why are light-coloured clothes particularly suitable for summer?

2 They reflect heat
   Dark clothes absorb more
   heat

1 Cooler (probe 'Why?')
   Get too dirty in winter

0 Look pretty in sunshine
   Thinner

17. Why does freezing food preserve it for a longer period?

2 Bacteria are less active at
   low temperatures

Stops bugs from spreading
1 Kills all the germs
0 Keeps the flies off
Tastes better when it is
cold

1 Radar
Very sensitive hearing
0 It can see in the dark
Knows its way around the
cave

**18. Why do flowers tend to
be brightly coloured ?**

2 To attract insects (who
help with pollination)
These are the ones we have
bred and chosen to
cultivate
1 Good for survival of plant
(probe 'How ?')
0 So they look pretty

**19. What causes tides at the
seaside ?**

2 Gravitation of the Moon
and Sun
The pull of the Moon as it
goes round and round
the Earth
1 The Sun's gravity
The Moon
0 The sea coming in
A full moon
Strong winds offshore
Rivers getting flooded

**20. How does a bat avoid
flying into things ?**

2 Emits noises which reflect
off obstacles
A kind of radar except
using sounds

**21. How does a submarine
dive under water ?**

2 Water pumped into its
tanks
Takes on some water
1 They make it heavier than
water (probe 'How ?')
0 They pull the periscope
down
They tilt the nose down
and rev the engines

**22. Why do we see a flash of
lightning a few seconds
before we hear the
thunderclap ?**

2 Light travels faster than
sound
1 The noise takes a long
time to get to us
0 The lightning happens
first
Our eyes work faster than
our ears

**23. Why does the Moon
change its shape ?**

2 We only see the part that
the Sun is shining on
Depends on angle of the

Sun in relation to our
viewpoint

1 Depends which angle we
view from
Sometimes eclipsed by
Earth

0 Clouds going past it
Sometimes it's full moon
and sometimes it's a new
moon

**24. If you were blindfolded
how would you know
what direction a sound
was coming from ?**

2 It would be louder on one
side than the other
The noise would reach
one ear sooner than the
other

1 Turn your head from side
to side

0 Listen hard
Peep under the blindfold
Ask somebody who could
see

**25. Why are rivers and
lakes less salty than the
sea ?**

2 Fed mainly by rainwater
which has evaporated
off/been distilled from
the sea leaving the salt
behind
Rivers constantly
refreshed by rainwater

1 Sea has been there longer
than the rivers
Salt accumulates in the sea
over time

0 There are salt mines at the
bottom of the sea
More fish in the sea

**26. Why does a compass
needle always point
north ?**

2 Earth's magnetic field
That is the direction of
north magnetic pole

1 Magnetism

0 Iron deposits under the
ground
Gravitation
Because the North star is
up that way

**27. How do ordinary
spectacles (glasses)
help some people to see
clearly ?**

2 They correct the faulty
focal length of the lens
in the person's own eye
so that images are better
focused at the back of
the eye (retina).

1 They help the person to
focus on things (probe
'How?')

0 Magnify things
Reduce eyestrain/glare

28. Why is mercury used in thermometers ?

2　It expands a great deal when heated

1　Very sensitive to temperature (probe 'In what way ?')

0　You can see it easily
　It looks pretty
　Very heavy

29. Why do we have seasons like summer and winter ?

2　Earth is tilted relative to the Sun and moves around slowly so that sometimes the North Pole is tilted towards the Sun and sometimes the South Pole

1　Earth is tilted
　Sun is higher in the sky in summer

0　Sun is further away in winter
　Because we go around the Sun
　Sometimes the Sun is on the other side of the Earth
　It would get boring if there were no seasons

30. Why does the Moon not fall down to Earth like an apple falling off a tree ?

2　Earth's gravity offset by centrifugal force due to orbital motion

1　In stable orbit (probe 'What does that mean exactly ?')

0　It's too far away for Earth's gravity to affect it
　God keeps it up there so it won't get too dark at night

Scoring for Test IV

Add up the number of points obtained according to the scoring codes given with the questions and refer the total to the table below to arrive at a 'science quotient'. Refer to the last chapter for interpretation of this quotient.

SCIENCE QUOTIENTS

SCORE	AGE 5*	6	7	8	9	10	11
0	80—	78—	76—	74—			
2	88	85	82	78	76		
4	95	92	87	83	80	76	
6	103	97	92	87	83	79	76
8	117	104	97	92	86	82	78
10	127	116	103	96	90	85	80
12	135	127	114	100	94	88	83
14	142	135	123	108	98	92	86
16	146	142	133	118	102	95	88
18	149	147	140	127	110	98	90
20	153	151	146	135	118	102	94
22		154	151	143	127	108	96
24			156	149	136	115	99
26				154	143	123	103
28					150	130	108
30					158	141	116
32						152	123
34						161	130
36							140
38							153

* Use this column for age range 5 yrs 0 mths to 5 yrs 11 mths.

Test V: Pattern completion

This test consists of a series of patterns in which the bottom right square has been left blank. Ask the child to complete the pattern by drawing in the design which he thinks should go there. If he does not get the idea you may demonstrate by filling in the first item. Thereafter do not prompt or tell him whether he is right or wrong. There is no real time limit but if after several minutes the child is obviously stuck he may be encouraged to guess and go on to the next problem. The problems get progressively harder as they go on; when the child begins to encounter difficulty he should be told this and reassured that later problems are really for older children. If he fails five successive items terminate the test.

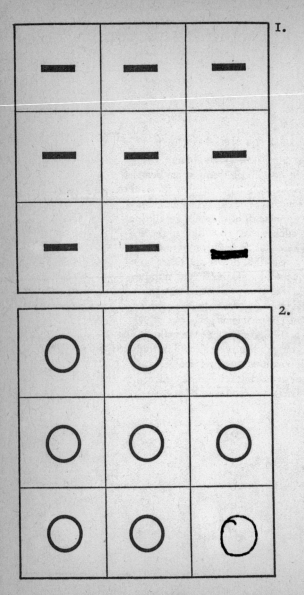

3.

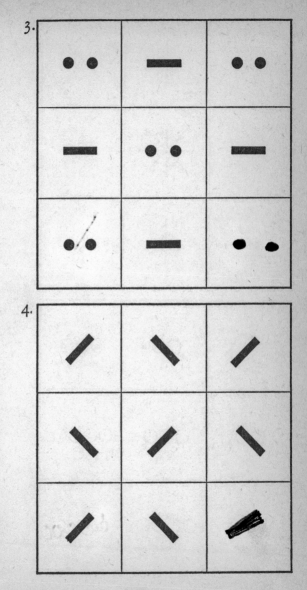

4.

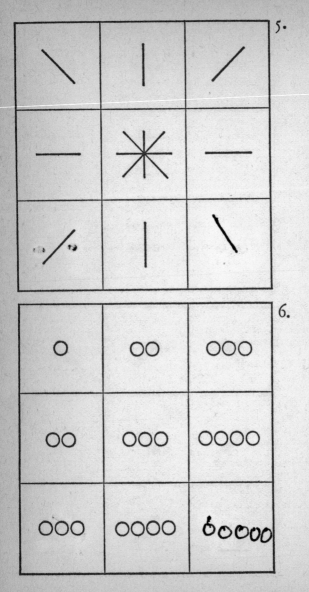

5.

6.

7.

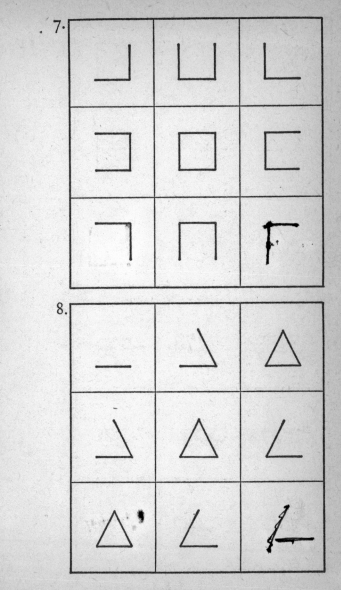

8.

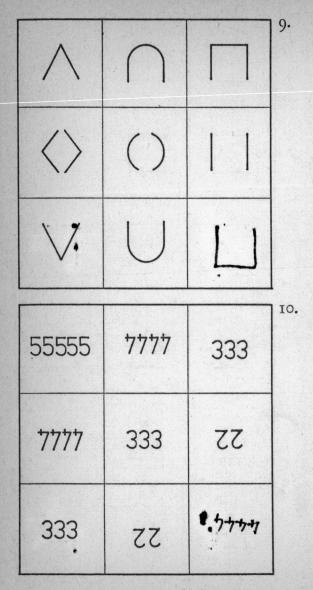

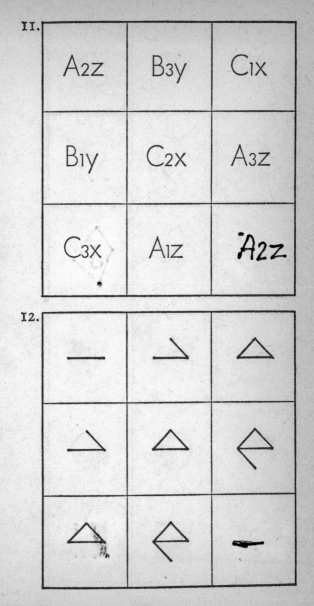

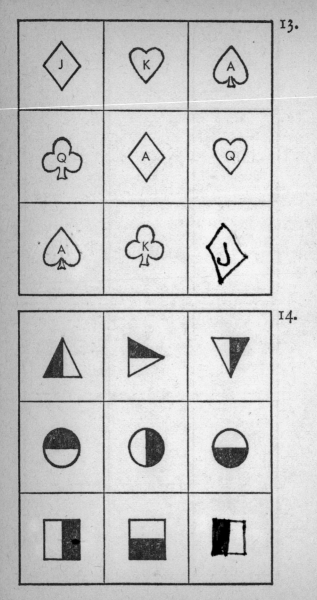

13.

14.

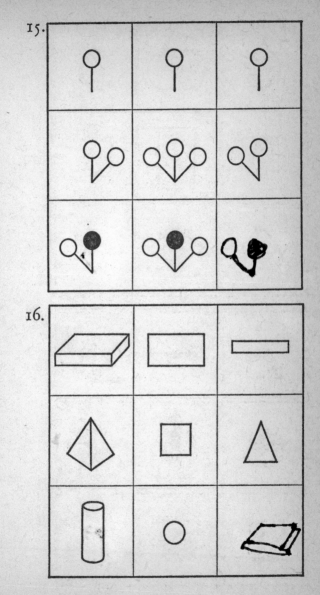

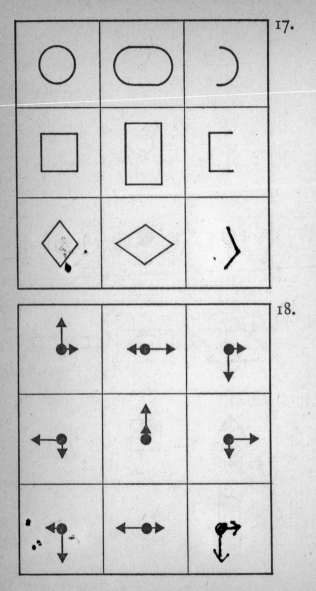

17.

18.

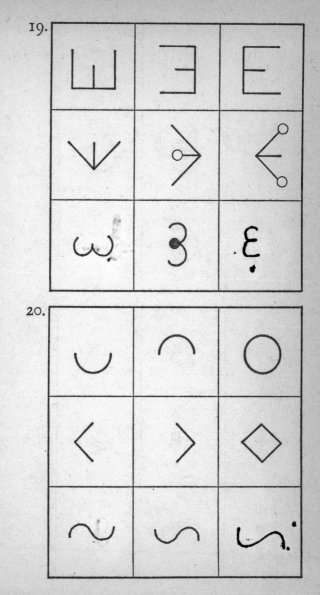

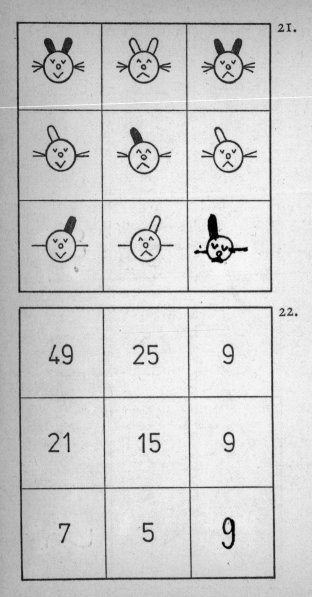

21.

22.

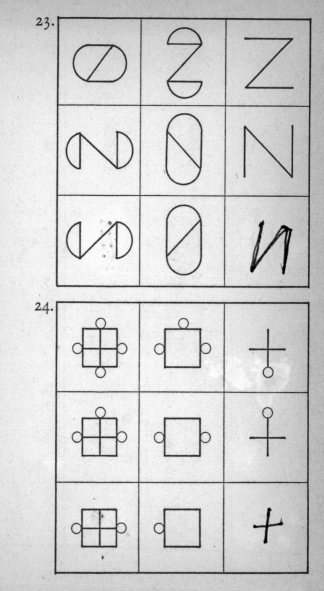

23.

24.

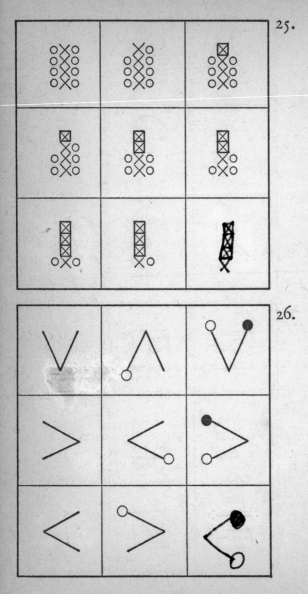

25.

26.

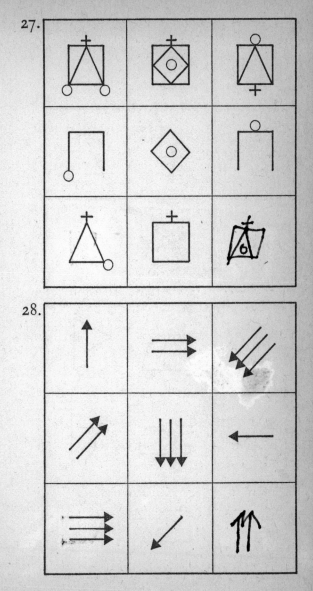

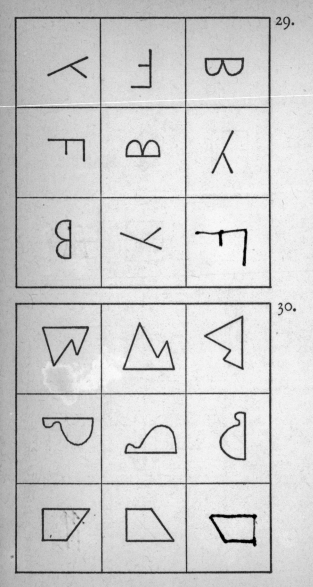

29.

30.

Scoring for Test V

CORRECT ANSWERS ARE:

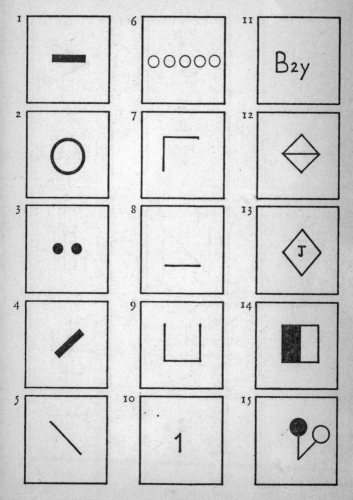

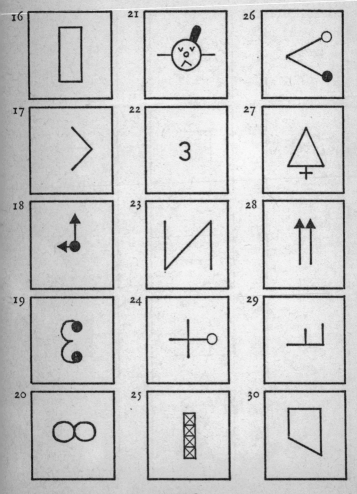

Add up the number of correct answers and refer the total score to the table below to arrive at a 'pattern quotient'. Refer to the last chapter for interpretation of this quotient.

PATTERN QUOTIENTS

SCORE	AGE	5*	6	7	8	9	10	11
0			70—	70—	70—			
1			80	80	80	70		
2			90	87	85	80	73	70	66
3			100	95	90	84	78	73	70
4			110	104	96	88	83	77	73
5			120	116	101	93	86	80	76
6			130	126	112	97	89	84	79
7			140	137	124	106	94	87	82
8			150	145	133	116	100	90	86
9				152	140	123	105	94	88
10					147	132	112	99	92
11					152	138	118	104	95
12						143	125	108	98
13						149	130	114	102
•14						152	136	120	107
15							142	124	112
16							146	128	116
17							149	133	120
18							152	137	125
19								142	130
20								145	134
21								148	138
22								152	142
23									146
24									149
25									152

* Use this column for age range 5 yrs 0 mths to 5 yrs 11 mths.

Interpretation of scores

Unless by now your child has torn up the book in frustration, you should have obtained five quotients, one for each of the five tests. These may be entered on the chart below by placing crosses at appropriate positions in the five columns. The five crosses may then be linked together with straight lines to give what might be called an 'intelligence profile'.

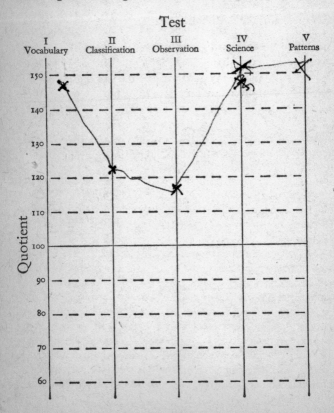

It will now be possible to see at a glance where the child's scores lie in relation to the average (represented by the 100 line). The best estimate of the child's overall IQ is the median of the five scores, that is the score that falls in the middle if the five quotients are put in rank order. For example, if the five quotients are 112, 110, 102, 85 and 80 then the child's IQ will be 102. This is preferred over the usual method of calculating an average for several reasons, one being that it takes less account of the extremes. The meaning of the IQ is explained in some detail in the introduction to the book but in general terms it may be interpreted as follows:

Above 140	Very superior	*156/5/148 12= 118*
120–140	Superior	
110–120	High average	
90–110	Average	
80–90	Low average	
70–80	Borderline	
Below 70	Mentally retarded	

People who achieve success in higher education and who enter the professions nearly always have IQs in the superior or very superior bands. An IQ in this range does not guarantee success in those fields – various other attributes such as interest and application are also important. The high level IQ does, however, seem to be a fairly necessary prerequisite. Some occupations typical of lower levels of intelligence are given in the introduction.

The five individual quotients can be interpreted in a similar way. In each case the average is 100 and the normal range is 80 to 120 (around three-quarters of the population falling between these points). These quotients are less reliable than the overall IQ – based as they are on a smaller sample of performance less confidence can be placed in their stability. However, bearing this reservation in mind, we can make some suggestions about what the profile might reveal. If the profile line is high on the left side in particular (vocabulary and classification higher than scientific understanding and pattern completion) the child probably tends to be strong in linguistic/verbal skills rather than logical, spatial and numerical. Such a pattern is found slightly more often in girls than boys and is characteristic of people who enter occupations such as teaching, journalism, social work, diplomacy and secretarial work. The reverse pattern, with the profile line climbing upwards from left to right indicates a relative strength in spatial, numerical and scientific reasoning. This is more characteristic of boys and lends itself to occupations such as engineering, research, driving, navigation, design and computer operation. Thus the shape of the profile line may give some indication of the relative strengths and weaknesses of the child. Note that the differences between the quotients should be at least 20 points before any degree of reliability can be assumed. Even then they should be interpreted with caution unless they vary systematically in the manner described above, i.e. a fairly consistent inclination from right to left or left to right.

Apart from the above verbal-spatial dichotomy, which is perhaps the most fundamental differentiation in IQ testing, there are some other possible causes of striking profiles. A language deficit of some kind, for example if the child's first language is not English, would result in a depression of the vocabulary, classification and perhaps also scientific understanding scores. This handicap should be obvious to the parent or tester even if they are not familiar with the child's background. Of course, in this case relatively non-verbal quotients will give a better indication of the child's true IQ. Certain kinds of brain damage will interfere more with the pattern completion and observation tests than with vocabulary and classification but these tests are not geared for making diagnosis of this kind, and anyway that should be left to professional psychologists and neurologists.

Hopefully, both parent and child will have gained some benefit from this book. The parent will know the child better – how his intelligence ranks with that of other children, and what are his strengths and weaknesses. The child should benefit both from this knowledge and from the experience of working through all the puzzles, which are very similar in format to those found in the most widely used IQ tests. (An exception is the scientific understanding test which is something of an innovation but believed by us to deal with an important area of intellectual development that has been sadly neglected in traditional tests.) At the end, we feel a responsibility to stress certain dangers with the use of this book:

1. Allowance needs to be made for a certain margin of error in all IQ tests. Child IQ tests are less reliable than adult IQ tests and the younger the child is when tested the less certain we can be about the validity of the result. With this book there is an important additional source of error – the inexperience of the tester. To some extent the child is helped or penalized by the tester's failure to administer and score the tests in exactly the correct manner. At the extreme we fear that a normal or bright child may be labelled as mentally retarded because the parent has horrendously misinterpreted the instructions or scoring tables. Therefore we urge that if any concern has been created by the outcome of these tests, or if any life decisions are to be based on them, the results should be checked by a qualified vocational psychologist. Such experts have better validated batteries of tests at their disposal and are properly skilled in using them.

2. If your child is confirmed as having a disappointing low IQ, do not accuse him of being lazy or inattentive at school. A low IQ tells you nothing at all about how hard the child has tried. It merely tells you that he is disadvantaged as regards his chances of showing academic superiority. In no way is he to blame for this disadvantage. Also, it is important to stress that an IQ is not a measure of a child's worth. Many other attributes such as courage, reliability, emotional stability, sense of humour, sincerity, love and kindness are every bit as important. These qualities are quite unconnected with superior intelligence, and often a great deal rarer. As someone has said, it's nice to be important but it's more important to be nice. And remember that there are many specialized talents such as sporting, musical and artistic

143

abilities which are also fairly independent of intelligence. IQ tests are not able to detect the future Olympic gold medallist nor even the budding creative genius. So do not berate your child for any deficiencies these tests may seem to have exposed. Look to his positive characteristics, whether intellectual or otherwise, and give him the support that he will need to develop them to the fullest.

Recommended reading

H. J. EYSENCK, *Know Your Own IQ*, London, Penguin 1962.
H. J. EYSENCK, *Check Your Own IQ*, London, Penguin 1966.
G. D. WILSON, *Improve Your IQ*, London, Futura 1974
H. J. EYSENCK AND G. D. WILSON, *Know Your Own Personality*, London, Penguin 1976.